How Many More of Them Are You?

How Many More of Them Are You?

Lisa Lubasch

Avec Books
Penngrove

I thank the editors of the following publications in which poems first appeared: *Boulevard*, *Explosive*, *The Hat*, *Boomerang!* and *An Avec Sampler Two.* L.L.

ISBN: 1-880713-19-5

Library of Congress
Catalog Card Number: 99-95210

First Edition

Cover photograph by Francesca Woodman,
used with permission from The Estate of Francesca Woodman.

Cover Design by Colleen Barclay

Avec Books
P.O. Box 1059
Penngrove, CA 94951

for Lois and Richard Lubasch, for my friends, and for all my teachers

Contents

I

How Many More of Them Are You?

15

II

On Decency

29

III

45

IV

63

V

79

VI

On the Value of Sin and Omission

87

*

Yesterday evening March 13th Yvonne's party.
Children of the quickening little stick.
The Etruscan clay pot.

—*Antonin Artaud*

*

the days go by. the outdoor world would hum “I too am false.”   or

*

“what is my deception?”

an ellipsis intuiting its form.

I

How many more of them are you?

*

If I declare *that* is what I am to answer for (do I dare?), the generals and juries will come out from their wine cellars (most with their wet-caps on) and cry, "That is enough! I have heard enough!" Insolent prudes! Embellishing the past with your pale sympathies! Man will discover signs before he ever has designs to read the sunset.

*

O empty flower. Breeder of life and of time. Suffer up your sadness like the bees.

*

I have no patience. I want to leave this life very quickly in order not to be barbered by its

*

Beauty is it legendary dead. Delinquent bird.

*

Slow hearse, (drifting) to the shore. Under the trudge-light, (death), the lesser phantom.

*

Does not some slender pole of reason still remain? Fancy is the feed-worm of the heart.

*

Dear   , that pitiful sloth which you call verse, etcetera. Down with the hatchet! The evil path of ecstasy doth never

allow.

*

Let us all murder one another.

*

Il n'y a que ces deux aspects—la raison et l'infini.

*

O single censured soul. Time is the miserable organ of time.

*

The eternal watchman has his charm. Surtout quand il me dit, “je me sens rejeté par la vie.”

*

ou   “Personne ne m’attend. Personne.”

*

O vile and sophisticated burglars of the night.   These are all *my* incantations!

*

Of a sun that searches out its prey, then buries it, I say “Deceptive sunlight! Implacable sidewalk! (Barren amour).”

Notes for a love poem to

*

for what my poems is.   apotheosis of decay.

*

rid me of these relics, words.   come to me and fuck me so I feel.

*

I will keep to myself. I will water my words with the plants of decay. speak only to the birds. (i'll close my ears.) I will not hear the failure of my

*

say.   all life is.   the febrile unity of firs.

*

on this imperious day, I write to you   unknown, unlovely, and unable.

*

these scars (of you), where all our gestures were
our wormed-desire, wet

(unentered).

*

for what it is that holds these lines (together)   if not for the lame hand of incertitude.

*

and swallowed my landscape hair   you left.

*

unexit.

(NOTE)

*

Amidst the junipers and ruins I will brutalize myself in meager forms.

*

(the degenerate will rasp   my arms.)

*

My words are memories of themselves. I revere them for the error which produces them. Namely that they are not as such.

(The faculty of having   one   submit.)

*

The beauty of discrepancies,   to sleep through our own pilgrimage . . .

*

No. love resembles all great forms of torpor,   writing its one page endlessly.

*

the days go by. the outdoor world would hum “I too am false.”

*

or "what is my deception?" the word is an ellipsis

intuiting its form.

*

I am not unlike an open wall, revealing as it opens back, its own immense unself. I am endeavor to describe both wall and what is opened into the where of its recession.

*

not order or idea, but motion is I its own imperative?

(Note)

A beautiful error invents me. That of my own fist.

(O night. the wind's amphibious drift.)

*

and if I say that I is just a series of elisions. that you is my (spastic) desire to contain "you," to continue *you.* what is my example?

*

(somewhere in this is the failure of abstraction. I too am damned.)

*

the horse, the broomstick, and the beam, the ineluctable odor of (something). why do I move through this trail? to repeat its error? to have this (error) order me?

*

O infinite solicitude of song.

*

What does it matter?   I will not here.

*

Positioning, repositioning in relation to the life. I a system of repulsions. I this averse condition is. Unremediable.

*

to say attractions are   the virile collusion of cruelties,

*

hand reciprocating fist. I this alliance.   fulcrum whereby life is formed.

*

I am not a part of this. that I, in comparison, is.   that's all.

*

I grow pious with imposture.

*

(You) the incapacity for naming   you.

*

This incomplete illogic which creates me.

*

I wish I could content myself in this house of figurative passions.

*

I is the process of an endless

*

No. Somebody must still stand for love's eventual.

II

On Decency

(Note)

I am rushing to write this   secrecy

spores

in the sores of our hands,

in the ears of our mind.

*

And
I would be ready to say something not to
lose this too, but what is it, and how say it.

The next room
is falling through its window, lost to the onset
of some new bloom, pointing to awakening, not

ours. So
why not forego all that fog, and me be the one to enter
next time, and

race-off at irremediable speed,
possessed of summer—lover, we misinterpret
at each peak the punishment for falling,

the tolerable word *sorrow*

just a substitute, which exists, needless to say,
no more than the rest of us beetles
down here, dreaming

indecency.

*

Odd
token of loneliness, this
remaining.

Moths in white circumference
round the room, some green entreaty to go home—hence
the question, "If I go home, where

will I be coming *from?*" and your sudden disappointment
that the wind, like an entire season
lowed out into the long expanse of

"seem." Keeps you decadent and
sinister. Which is the way your love is anyway.
Simulacrum.

*

It's like the (sayable), all sudden
gone with the huntsman (who *was* beautiful), off
on the road to some gross oneliness, sad

roamable future. No, not about hour
but time, and the more you condone
each wreckage, the more you become (sum total of) its parts,

a traveler cast out by the very ruined forms that you imagined
were your own—
                        indecent trees, depicting some pale scene of

course, vagrancy has its pros
("in a sense"), and
            I am some diction of the dead

relevance of that love, castrated
like a kind of looking
where what matters is the object we

suppose—some stiffish wind, an insoluble
jutting, and

                            the *and* that keeps harvesting
contingencies (rain). Not to efface the natural
boundaries to
                            imagine them.

*

And the punishment continued. But who really asked us
if anything we rigged-up flew, fell off, or
followed

forth, forthwith
or without what you knew—how

each of our intentions has abstracted its own
chaos from among the holdings, from each
forgiveness, something invaluable

lost, some capacity for, what is it, naming
greed, rancor, some system of tenable
nevers . . .

Is it part of the philosophy of flex
and surrender, the limp of your withdrawal
like a (   ) claim

to the number of possibilities
for the way back, as if you could have even one
encumbered vision of a dawn,

dutifully recognizing its light
less and less, like the day *it* surrenders, however
valiant the upsurge.

*

Maybe it is tomorrow.

Warped lodge, truant house,
summer's statics of containment.
But what's happened to the entrances?

And where is that thin lark now?

And can one really stop
turning around the expansive
seam, crawling it,

hobnailed,
in the garden that utilizes darkness
sometimes well.

*

Something of that long vehement escape
has rested with (me) here,
even with that fille long far gone,

whom you left, appropriately, looking at her cat
you began hating, with just a thin blue rue
along the rue of the divide, what it was

you wanted to get at.
An unknowable liturgy?
Ach! This prison is a country,

the fury of its muse like a very old fog
you would move through
if you could find it, the air

a long-drawn pause in the damp
recitation, identifiable
because it moves like fear,

spits and curs and comes up (   ) for air.

*

          There is, in despair, a great blue lump
of clotted form, some nefarious fiction
you insisted was your own, some dull excruciate

that is your animate. Mounting each other on the road,
you felt a longing infidelity
to light, the fulgurating rhythm of light

and (incongruous) love, grown out of its trees, out
over the neat blue hills, removed
from the suffering others who

set down their hats and saw lights
in monuments . . .

*

But there are things one cannot live with.
The points of departure,
thick with their infernos and dried weeds.

And there are things one cannot
leave—the lovely indecorous throat
between ranges of fingers and

the thing that's never emerging,
that wants to see its own reflection in the fog
going back, calcareous, among rocks.

Can we be convinced that there is more?

(and that huntsman out loping round
the host of the unknowable . . .)

*

You didn't understand the terms.
The thin vamp of that fog, another
language which keeps on . . .

But what do you do when it comes to this?
And this? Isn't it enough
that the wind keep towing?

The lightest attachment draws us in-
finitives. The stiff-worn summit of
it seems . . .

Clayed long ago, another room,
back of its house, still writes
its letter out, rough wind

arriving in arms.

*

Imagine
who this is written to anyway,
at the beautiful end of some consumptive

margin, wall of its awakening
tip of
pale utterance,

proffering arms.

And what *of* the flowers?
Do they really seek to revise
(destiny), and if they do, what dead

spring will give its secret
to decay, sun of another room,
day no longer.

*

. . . the ugly seduction of *were* or the failing of
we—not *our*, *I'm*

and the more you condone.   each wreckage.
your progenitor.   some total of your parts.

an outcast traveled by the very ruined forms that had imagined you
their own.   cyanotic

trees, blue itinerant
guise.   of course vagrancy.

am I some

fiction of the dead love
of that relevance

looking

a kind of (contingency)
pain that keeps harvesting

its ends. (castrated). all gone
sudden. with the (if not to efface the)

huntsman—

(Note)

Outside, the leaves bluster across their ars poetica, coasting into one another, occasionally catching, getting caught inside the snare of some low bush.

It's the problem of traffic, of who is claiming what, of what is to be thought of or perceived . . .

"Matter as the wish to complete itself,"

ground, the grassy layer flayed, revealing lichens, mosses, stunted shrubs—
a tundra of meaning.

The sovereign in between
what happens and what happens—

a day not even a day
but that first and last idea in which we.

(NOTE)

Blue malignant flowers hung in caps
along the fissures of the everglade.

Huskily flowers now curl now conceive
of the wind, must pitilessly
make themselves resist

green light struck along the importunate fog.

Now presently now done,
the light goes down
in slackening folds and

curiously bent down over the tall grasses, I.

"The word for this is flight."

In the road where you have just
parted, it is all figures
and the gulf between them

and this.

III

("Quiet night, quiet night. Especially nowhere sung.")

The Last Supplicant ("to a God")

What I mean is—having come to—
having come to—a procession—having meaning
as the option—

I vanish behind a tree

the light, dividing, slowly opens
into this spared flower

what is it that you
discourage me from seeing?

*

if a shape brightens, it is to redefine itself, which may involve a de-identification with the social world around it—this is not to dignify itself—it is to call attention to its flight.

*

I grow anemic and ingrown. I begin to miscreate myself.

*

a great fatigue unnames me.

*

if a shape brightens,   is it to miscreate itself?

*

(my sickness is a presence in the world.   your music is solicitous.)

*

to clay away at life, as if to lacerate its ear.

*

these meanings that I hoard. disintegration is.

Leprosarium

1

The door is at the wind. The bargeman knocks not twice   but in and out me of her spirit roars. *Si vous me touchez . . . tu ne risques rien.*   Infidèle! Infidèle! In fi   dèl   e!

2

O mildewed lady of the sidewalk! Barren years and yours   are the fuming eyes of.

3

I have gone outside again. The anthills make me sick.   Ci vil I zay tion!   "CE QU'IL FAUT . . . !"

4

what is it that in your eyes I hear?   (your eyes)   remembered like a cane. endemic. ancillary. blue.

5

Beauty is it legendary dead.   Delinquent bird.

(Note)

*

I am hungry, Joseph Harbinger. Can you not even offer me some pain?

*

(Je meurs de faim.   Je n'ai même pas faim.)

1

Enough!!! I will not stand in line and gawk and gabble like a goon! If the soul speaks, then that's that. And that *is* everything. And by extension, why are we always asked to hear a song just to get at the wrong note? So what of the redhead in the supermarket? Shouldn't we put our carrots in a basket first? Shouldn't we choose a basket? Take the *fromage* and head for home! . . . Why this lingering?! This commiserative clutch of cackling cloons! Ordering the soul's mad music isn't everything.

2

You've got rhododendrons in my pockets and a pocket full of verse. I'll be kissing in the snow when you come home. Your majesty!

3

July! Wisteria! Monseigneur's tower is hot! *Dear Mnemosyne, so delighted with these interruptions . . .*

4

Oh my darling, can't we go away and be at once in love?   In one white word—come—back. It's early. Must I fix myself in milk-and-water rhyme so soon? One more hour and Merganser will take a fish. Can't I have one too? Must I admire endlessly?

4a

Mercury, take this message.

5

I am a dried-up prune in a Cartesian universe. Today I left my love inside the longhouse on the lake . . . playing rummy. With whom? Sacrée fille! Wearing slopwork from Belgrade.   A carrot's on my heel. Ah more delightful than most philosophies in France. Were it cooked correctly! Hippocrene, take this oath. Feel my lips. I am dry.

6

Morning. The first eye opened. Outside in search of eggs, the city hot. (Salad days?)   Moreover, I am convinced that Joan of Arc once did something here.

7

My darling, with you I'm but a basking shark. Are you the sun? Must I die knowing that you saw me squint?

8

Come—let me see your loose shirt lift. We are so uneasy this way, side by side, with our chrestomathy laid out on the linoleum. Picasso! *We have little film so please work fast!* S'il vous plait. *Oui, ça me plait.* That's the idea. Coupez.

9

Now that spring has come, can we let go and wander to and fro between the panicles and pines? Or must we move the way these thorns are rising on their stems?

10

Fools we are who fancy that our flowerage is important. Were I to doze all day indoors, not one fine libertine would dip her head in to restore me!

Note. *Folie à deux.* Picasso *could* eat a fish without disturbing any of its bones.

11

Think don't think. Imagine yourself in the fall. Is it spring? There is snow on the ground. Is there not? If you think. *Pensez. Entre nous,* a word is a bestial thing.

12

Isn't this a disappointment, love. This that once I thought you were have you turned out to be notatall. Have you overheard my hasty *screaming in the heat?* Or has some hoyden harnessed your attention? Had we played hare and hounds, I'd have pursued your papers strenuously. Illuminati! Tell! I have inhaled high clouds and exhaled.

13

In my fever, I work to dissolve meanings. Does nothing around me beckon to be said but that which has already attained a graceful petrification in the mind? We being as such (petrified), we must prepare to follow forth with more than faithful forms.

A man comes running at me wearing a suit and a tie. Do I hinder his progress? Do I present myself as a great barricade? Do I question him?! Yet he is my fate.

Sometimes, if I am in sore need, I will ask "do you have a pencil?" Today la dame replied "it's eleven ohhh three." Thank you.

14

Do you not know that I conceal each time I cry "Life is a spectacle!" You there behind the window, let's have a look at *your* "changing face."

15

Dear   , been thinking of declaring you *inconsequent.* And concerning the distinction between bad art and the rest. No, I've not a thing to help. Sincerely, sansunn om.

*

This is what I think, Lisa. I think this relationship is no good for you because it stirs up evil in your bones. No more feeling the poplars out. The past is a blue frigate. Or nothing.

*

At last! A list of life transgressions. Carrying the wind home went too far. I should have stayed that shortcut on.

*

to which the meter could not cry, o'er
which the reiner could not rein. Restrain
the gigantesque, the grotesque eloquence of song,
and make this verse

terse.

*

Stop mourning the loss of the past! Propriety is *better* past and done. What do we want with, anyway, the past,   if all it is, or we are,   (are we?) gone.

*

Bagh! I too am angry now! Good riddance to you darlin' (E.), now get yourself a goin'.

*

and what of the law student who kicks himself in the ars for desiring anything different?!

*

Come home and hear the horses roar. Like the desert lion.

*

Heal bird. Dote on the dates and figs of
Hear the   ?

*

The day belongs to what I've called *a human thought.*

*

My wife has stolen my left shoe. The bitch had the braggart bury it.

*

each endeavor carelessly broken, carelessly broken and alone. I crave indifference like a calf.

*

Fool who brings his fodder up only to bring same food back down.
Fool who brings his fodder out only to find one horse to feed.
In any herd of cattle, there are at least (two) who've got chutzpah.

Fancy that.

*

Hypocrisy! The wagon wheel must turn.   Remembering that old Italian bitch, I too can cry "Putain! Sciolism sucks me dry!"

*

to which the meter could not cry, o'er
which the reiner could not rein. Restrain
the gigantesque, the grotesque eloquence of song,
and make this verse

(terse).

*

Je suis toute seule avec

*

When I suffer, singing "I am the rogue," it is not as nice as all that.______________________________

*

I have no memory of dust
but what I know of incantation—

*

(My reflection in the dirt
is not a reflection.)

IV

"I want to sleep
laid into a vacancy
like eyes."

(NOTE)

for all the widening flora of your words,   this tundra of.

*

I am sick with what I cannot say.

*

That I have marked these tantric places with my hands, so that you will have known that I've existed.

*

I am not the sole transcriber of my lonelinesses.

*

Lovers far away. Wet symbols of my soul's serous indifference. I have felt your muted substance. I am thick with it.

*

(elsewhere I have claimed love entire.)

*

I am prolixity and passion,   paramour and pact.   the symbol of an act, whereby the act is ill-imagined, the symbol, inexact.

*

My exhaustion qualifies me.

*

wherever I am, I am its understanding.

*

it is mine.

*

In its decay, the world unsings. I am the mate of this collapse.

*

(disease   has kept my vile love of it intact.)

*

Exhaustion revels in itself, revealing I am nothing but form.   I would become that nothing (almost) instantly. This degeneration appeals to my sense of endeavor. Sew less of the morning into me. So that I may unravel faster.

*

I dare not say that I am. imposture would go something then like this.

*

In persisting do I fail to (see).

*

response is not an answer.

*

In seeking , I seek myself instead. This sickens me. Of all great words we write the few that steady in our ear and still. Indicted by progression are the sounds we do not hear.

*

I will not say instead.

*

Aggressor and disgraced appraiser of my doubt, I am my own unword

*

admonishment of this, my human soul

*

I have, I fear.

*

(That evil should succumb to the fastidiousness of Nature's quiet forms,

*

that evil should spring from itself, not fully, only desperately), —

*

Everything is saddened by anticipation (of it),

*

by its prodigious form, by its excess.

*

The word traverses me.

(Note)

*

It's not the graying field of grass that signifies decay

*

nor the withered field becoming white

*

but the still-green insurgents ennobling the lawn

*

this (love) that lashes out at me, unrestful (like an ear).

*

And of the convalescent who turns his freakish back upon decay. Affronte tes maladies. Il faut les embracer.

*

O greenish man of health

were you and I
the leaf upon my thigh

*

So like a pair of shears to rive the endless, so unlike (a gourd).

*

The cautious cleave to one another with their wet electric hair. O mad ecstatic poetry. the burning faggot of my (heart).

*

O sinful vehicle of (life),   would I were a word.

*

if I could ever keep my thoughts contagious,   their indentures I would spread

*

to words I would have turned myself eternal,   mordant, not immortal.

*

O primitive cattle. Turned inside your pimpled hides. When will we come out and cry "God save us *and* the horses!"

*

No more. Throw heroic deeds into the dirty den of "progress." Empiricism goes to the

*

prostitute of the decade! Méfie-toi! Evil is the carbuncle of pleasure's parted (cunt).

*

C'est quoi ce *truc* là? Rien.

*

(Et ce sera demain quand je ressentirai tout ça.)

*

like our forbears, the Great Whitefeet   summon up the snow.   The nose of our next noose is rolling naked on the hearth.

*

Behind the fortress we are birthed   grievous like a goat.

*

Prostitute of the decade. Méfie-toi.   Words are a moaned desire   for words.

*

but

*

if all the widening flora were your words

*

in maimed unpleasant places,

*

sick precipitants of song,

*

the muted vain refusal of our words

*

to fall

*

together

*

the shift of incessant creation.

*

Of the man who, being worn, leads you through the leaves unlike a bear. Beware. O

sanctimonious beast of brutal virtue.

(Note)

rain in the spasm of your chest

the river's blue heathen my love is

virgin scabs on cows' white udders.

V

Narcotic bloom of leaf—
what you wanted to give me.

*

keeping in it. edges to itself. the bed more like escarpment

than wave. the hand, mutating fingers, angle of entrance 33 degrees
and one long torpor of. everything growing old, sloughing away
adjacencies, flora pouring out of

so many directions, how to keep one
solid, in the body, even though rheumatic, how to root it
in a form,

bilious, digging, sickening into it,
purulent, though light, half-rising
through the fore,

a stiffish wind, an insoluble jutting,
situating line along the low expanse of leaves. As if
this were a wood,

the wind, a difficult litany—

*

As if everything that had stopped being charted
had been left to develop its own course, been left

to fatten, fill, fill out
into an ordonnance of forms, drawing out of it

a long cold sleep of days
without dissolve, everything drained and renewed

in terms of its own . . .

*

neither forest nor field
but both, though the idea

of either lost

to the one big hole
which it resembled

more often than night
in the fresh blue light of the low

sum of days, the blue rot of days,

the long blue light of the vaporous days,
which was, several in its streams, retreating,

*

which is to say, what the body meant to have
its fields reopened, to give up its notes, finally

to have everything
gone, intricacies of border, gone

everything slaked off, shorn, shorn off
into enceinte.

*

the jutting body, pale, recusant, jutting, not pale
like flesh, but antic, ludicrously

pale, unmanned,

*

in its hole

*

the swift blue sound of sleep
molting over it,

*

bellying its emptiness like days
belie their fullness ("everything blue, everything green")

wanting to get at meaning, wanting to mean
exactly

a long and untouched terror (stricken into sound
like the error it resembles),

a voice in the next room,
("oh if only to hear this much of your voice . . .
can only hear this much of . . .")

something other than itself to give
it sound, limit . . . something

entrenchable

*

in its hole

*

fabled into being like the body it became
utterance, entranced, genital,

stirred, stirred up
birds, their wings torped wide in triangles,

spur-winged, wagging, wagged
into these words

poured out in rains, acred

urgings towards vergency.

*

the heresy of morning . . . that its loose sheet should fit around the body of the room. her hair is ferns, her body is its detritus.   seizure of lips.   obeisant gesture of. the ache of their dissension still unformed.

*

I am serotinous cadaver of my own suspended death,   its bloom,   the lovely incontrovertible rhyme of

*

ornate and bannered leaves.   You are least unlike a scene of your own fall

*

its sequences still, as yet, unstarted—in all its orgiastic detail, love and hoard.

VI

(On the Value of Sin and Omission)

(On the value of sin and omission)

a rotting out of objects is a form

to the extent that poetry reinforces what it seems to know of treason

so must we make amends with all dead forms

for I am an interpretation of nature

take for instance, the soul

change bears slow resemblance to the word

must only be   concerns be   the object be

the still-born words of our last

(take for instance).

*

Nor have we been haphazardly construed as the winged aggressors of our sleep. The success of gravity's systems in doling out punishments for flight has all but killed the maimed pursuer of its forms.

*

for what the casual reducer does to form is satisfy himself with pure imperatives.

*

"All forms of life are in me final,"

*

"My dream precedes me. My imagination imagines me."

*

to punish the wind for its impotence,

*

or, to lengthen the beautiful emptiness decrepitude,

*

not being heard out over inveterate evening, (little bird)—

*

these lepers are my friends.

*

"A great lumbago tames the orator who strains himself at night into the apish and unkind, memorizing beautiful positions of his pain."

*

"To sleep beneath ourselves in sleep.   to exorcise the spirit of (   ) negation."

*

"We are all victims of symmetry and designs thereof. the panting summits, green excesses, scoliotic forms. the grottoes that have hollowed out the plains of   (my) development."

*

"If only to pursue continuum.   Am I waiting to be told?"

*

"But how to wait.   to figure form and pause . . ."

*

*

"No matter.   These abortive fragments are my homes."

*

"(misshapen province   solitude)"

*

"and if I arrive at the false margin of creation? —   the hinge of which is."

*

"Still. to ascribe a form to pause. I am convinced that what is fragmented and momentary is of the most intense value."

*

paranoiac (rain).   in the store-house, deep.   seed.   (me).

*

"I am not.   I do not   own things."

the thin-fall of a die.   does.

*

(the sick) attraction.   let fin let   fault-

*

line of (pain)'s various.

*

this I will undone.

*

"I should have (just) gone to sleep woken up like this with the rain at my back"

*

No. "the rain doesn't succumb to anything"

*

dark wood behind trees, transilient

imperturbable ground—something
not sourced, though constantly

sound,   outside the   hours . . .   instead

sin them.

*

the resinous

error resemblance,
a wandering of.

ands, surrounded by the.

(genitive).

*

(are we of
hands not being spoken,
or   not being

arms, are we
unsaid ?
each, this

de-articulation
of

)—

*

the apodictic rain, its reascent—

*

"but will you know
whom to trust, to maneuver
over the prostrated landscape with

whom to fall ?"

*

"I do not know. when the burnt leaf.
that you burnt.
was.   ever."

*

(in) deep deplorable arms, the wind goes out not once.

"heavy-world,   (interminable)"

(sound-like attenuating sound)—

*

despite "endless," I live
dark-eyed and numbered
in an alleyway of numbers, —

and all that pierces through the flesh of my ear is.

so what *of* the rain?

or

was that you in the door just now?

(serpent of the house that is not my house, —)

About the Author

photo by Dawn Blackman

Lisa Lubasch was born in New Rochelle, New York in 1973. She attended Yale University as an undergraduate and received graduate degrees from Johns Hopkins (MA, 1996) and The University of Iowa (MFA, 1998). She lives in New York City.